150 Facts About Grieving Children

By Erin Linn

The Publisher's Mark
P.O. Box 6300
Incline Village, Nevada 89450

To my son, Chris.

Written with brevity but profundity, this sensible book will be of enormous help to all professionals and parents in understanding the powerful and unique grief experiences of our children.

Rabbi Dr. Earl A. Grollman
Author: *Talking About Death: a Dialogue Between Parent and Child*

Erin Linn presents 150 facts about grieving children in a concise and easy to read fashion facilitating their incorporation into relations between adults and children experiencing the loss of a loved one. This book is an excellent basis for understanding a child's grief.

THANATOS

If you have a child or work with children, you have to have this book! The information is accessible and valuable to anyone who encounters a grieving child.

Darcie D. Sims
Grief Management Specialist, Author, Educator & Mom

A useful book for those unfamiliar with childrens' grief, written in a simple, direct style. Like the author's other books, this work is insightful and compassionate.

The Journal
Grief Education Institute

150 Facts About Grieving Children is a precise
collection of the latest grief information in simple terms.
I recommend this book be purchased for school libraries,
public libraries, and academic libraries.

Lynn Ossolinski
1990 President, Nevada Library Association
1989-90 Chair of Northern Nevada Governor's
Literacy Coalition Advisory Council

For those of us working with the grieving child
and for those of us wanting to come to a better understanding of this child, Erin Linn's book sheds additional
light.

Fernside
A Center for Grieving Children

I've just scanned the contents and can't wait to
curl up and read it from cover to cover. Looks like
another terrific resource that we can share with our
families, educators, and community.

Hospice of the Red River Valley

Caring for children who grieve requires great
sensitivity, warmth, and love. What do you say? How
do you respond? This book addresses many of the
important issues in a way that everyone can understand.

Stephen Ministries

Acknowledgements

To Rabbi Dr. Earl A. Grollman who encouraged me to write this book as a follow up to my first book, *Children Are Not Paper Dolls.*

To my son, Chris, who provided me with my own private research laboratory and opened my eyes to the pain of a grieving child.

To my son, Michael, who taught me that "butterflies may well be the little children of angels."

Preface

I have chosen to include quotes from two of my favorite books because they express my feelings in a way that I am unable to. The first of these books, *Although the Day is Not Mine to Give, I'll Show You the Morning Sun,* was given to me by my dearest friend since childhood. The book starts off by saying:

> "I look from the window to watch
> you playing in the yard,
> your bird's nest hair
> disarranged by changing winds
> and carefree days.
> Your sun-toasted face peers from
> beneath your tousled thatch.
> Quick, darting looks clear your vision;
> I see you dream your dreams."

This was me - many times - watching my two little boys play. Little did I know that all too soon one would be gone and the other would be forced into a life situation that was unknown and unthinkable - a child having to go through the pain and turmoil of grief.

Children do grieve, and with an intensity that would astound many adults. We cannot shelter them from death any more than we can take their grief away. But, we can obligate ourselves to learn more about child bereavement. We must begin to understand their world, their feelings, their hurts.

These short, concise facts are neatly organized, arranged, and presented as only an ex-
teacher turned part-time author would do. This
book will not provide you with everything you
ever wanted or needed to know about grieving
children . . . but it's a darn good start.

We all want to help our children, to be
there for them, to be able to say that we made
a positive difference in their lives. In closing,
the book, *Although the Day is Not Mine to Give,
I'll Show You the Morning Sun*, states:

> "Take my hand my child,
> and we will explore the land.
> I will tell you all that I know,
> and you will show me
> the secrets of the heart.
> It may not be a fair exchange,
> but it is all that I have to give."

Quotes from another of my favorite books,
The Prophet, are on the following pages.

On Children

And a woman who held a babe against her bosom said, Speak to us of Children.

And he said:

Your children are not your children.

They are the sons and daughters of Life's longing for itself.

They come through you but not from you,

And though they are with you, yet they belong not to you.

You may give them your love but not your thoughts.

For they have their own thoughts.

You may house their bodies but not their souls,

For their souls dwell in the house of tomorrow, which you cannot visit, not even in your dreams.

You may strive to be like them, but seek not to make them like you.

For life goes not backward nor tarries with yesterday.

You are the bows from which your children as living arrows are sent forth.

The archer sees the mark upon the path of the infinite, and He bends you with His might that His arrows may go swift and far.

Let your bending in the archer's hand be for gladness;

For even as he loves the arrow that flies, so He loves also the bow that is stable.

The Prophet
Kahlil Gibran

1 Death in a child's life is inevitable and unavoidable. The incidence of death experiences in children's lives is obvious. Almost every child will experience the death of a significant other, be it a pet, friend, or relative. More dramatically, about 1 out of 20 will experience the death of a parent by age 18. In an average-size school, about every 3-4 years, a child can be expected to die, affecting the lives of the child's friends, schoolmates, teachers and family.

2 Death means different things to children at different ages:
2-3 years - dead is just a word
4-5 years - partially understand
6-7 years - death is reversible
8 & up - a good understanding

Obviously, these ages of understanding may vary with the maturity of the child.

3 Young children (age 1-5) grieve more for the threat to their security; older children (age 6 & up) grieve more for the actual loss. Young children do not understand that dead is forever, and are more worried about who will take care of them now.

4 Children grieve differently at different ages. As they mature they have to *re-work* their grief. For example, a daughter will grieve differently at 13 for her mother who has died than she will at 25 when she has just had her first child and becomes a mother herself.

5 Our immediate instinct is to remove very young children from the home if a family member or close relative has died. Sometimes young children are kept from their parents for several hours or days and tended to by adults they are not familiar with or may not even know. This can cause a great deal of anxiety and confusion for a child.

6 Most children want to be included in the funeral arrangements, the funeral, and viewing the body. Children need to say their good-byes also.

7   Never force children to take part in death-related activities such as making them go to the funeral or cemetery or kiss grandma good-bye as she lays dying from cancer. But if children wish to do these things, by all means let them.

8   Generally speaking, it is easier for a child who has seen or been close to death to cope with it as opposed to a death that has taken place in another town or state. Viewing the body of the deceased is important for both adults and children to give them a sense of finality. It is especially hard if the body of the deceased is never found or recovered. There is always the nagging thought that maybe the person is still alive somewhere.

9   In most cases, children who view the body are glad they did. If adults do not give them the impression that it is horrible and morbid, children will probably do just fine. It may also answer a lot of questions they have but are afraid to ask, and we are afraid to answer.

10   Often children like to put some type of memento into the casket, and if they express a desire to do this, then they should be encouraged along these lines and aided in choosing an appropriate item. Anything from secret notes to pet rocks have been included, and this can give the child a great deal of satisfaction.

11 Children should be given the opportunity to keep at least one or several mementos of the deceased. So often the children are not even considered when the possessions are given out or given away. Even very young children will appreciate having something of the deceased one's belongings when they grow older.

12 Let children have some input as to how and when the room of the deceased will be *dismantled.* It can be very unnerving for them to come home one day and suddenly find everything gone.

13 Some children have a hard time going to the cemetery, and won't go even years after the death. Either it is too uncomfortable for them, too far away, or they just don't receive any comfort in doing so. Still others may find great comfort in going. This is a matter of preference and the wishes of each individual should be respected.

14 Older children should go to the cemetery by themselves if they wish. Some children do not like to go with their parents because they feel bad if their parents start to cry. Children don't like to see their parents cry. Period! End of story! But more importantly, this may be a very special, private time for the child to share with the deceased, and the child may really want and need to be alone.

15 Give children honest information about the death based on their level of maturity. Don't assume that children are too young to understand, and don't worry that they will be scarred for life by anything that you say to them regarding the death. They will process what they can understand, and what they can't understand will probably be brought up again by them at a later date.

16 Do not be afraid to tell a bereaved child the truth if you do not know the answer to some of his or her questions about the death. Don't make something up. The child will appreciate your honesty.

17 Do not use euphemisms with children. If grandfather died, tell the child grandfather died; not that he went away on a business trip or is taking the longest nap of his life. Always be truthful. Children can sense when something is gravely wrong, and will not trust you in the future if they find that you have lied to them. They can handle the truth.

18 Children may favor one parent over another to share their grief with. This should not make either parent feel bad, for the best interest of the child should be the prime concern.

19 Parents are often the hardest people for a bereaved child to talk to. Children are very protective of their parents and usually do not want to do or say anything that will cause them more tears or grief over a loss. Hopefully, if the child is not talking with the parents, the child is talking with someone else such as a friend, minister, school counselor, etc. It is advisable that children have someone available to them if and when they do want to talk.

20 It is important for the child that the family talk as a group about the loss, especially if the person who died is a close family member. Sharing memories is a healthy part of healing.

21 Even mature children need support from family and friends after a serious loss. Grief is not diminished by age.

22 To children, the divorce of their parents is very much like a death and will trigger the same type of grief that an actual death would. Also, moving to a new town or changing schools could be considered a serious loss even though no death is involved.

23 If children have lost a family member such as a parent or sibling, they will probably feel jealous of other families that are *complete*. The children may feel a need to complete this family by getting mom or dad a new mate or getting a new brother or sister. A child may feel that the person can be replaced as easily as a new pet.

24 When a child dies in a family, the adults have to deal with the death as well as the changed behavior of the other children in the family. The same is true for the bereaved siblings. They have to deal with the loss as well as the changed behavior of their parents.

25 Many children feel that their parents are nicer to them after a sibling dies. Sometimes parents can be nice to the point of being overindulgent, and this is not good for the child.

26 Some children may feel jealous of the attention the dead sibling gets from their parents' grieving and may feel unloved themselves. Or, they may be jealous of how much attention the bereaved parents get from others.

27 Holidays are very hard for grieving children . . . especially Halloween with its displays of ghosts, caskets, and skeletons. Many times parents try to over-compensate during holidays, and this can backfire. Let the children have input as to how the family will spend future holidays, at least for the next year or so. They will probably have some great ideas.

28 Parents who lose a child often become overprotective of re-maining children, and likewise bereaved children often become overprotective of their parents. Neither situation is healthy and can stifle the person being pro-tected. Because there is such a fear of more loss, one tends to suffocate those close to them.

29 Sometimes bereaved parents will become too *underprotective.* They despair at the idea that if they couldn't save one child, why beat their head against a wall, for no reason, trying to protect others. Thus, remaining children may not receive even normal care and concern for a time.

30 Children are often forced to use the coping behavior that their parents use, even though this way of coping may not be right or healthy for the child. For example, a parent may feel that the best way to cope with the loss is to remove all pictures and belongings of the deceased, whereas the child may find the grief work inhibited by being denied these items that give great comfort.

31 Children can sense that their parents are feeling paranoid regarding the child's safety. Children may have a feeling of being smothered or unable to make even small decisions regarding their well-being. This can affect the child's self-confidence, and the child may counteract by becoming openly rebellious or careless.

32 It is common for children to believe that the child who died was the *favorite* of their parents. They see their parents grieve so over the child who died and find it hard to believe that the parents would grieve just as much if they themselves died and their brother or sister lived. Thus, they may feel guilty that they lived and the favorite child died.

33 Unfortunately, it is sad but true sometimes that the child who died was the favorite child, and the parents make no bones about it. This is especially difficult for remaining siblings.

34 When a death occurs, children may see their parents - their pillar of strength - either crumble or withdraw before their very eyes at a time when they may need them most. It can be healthy for children to see their parents grieve so that they will know that grieving is normal and natural. But, it can be very scary for children to see their parents grieve, especially if the parents become so depressed they are unable to function in a way that the children are accustomed to. Parents need to be aware of ways in which their grieving may affect their child.

35 Children may become very frightened if it is the first time they have seen their parents cry. Although it may be difficult for the child at first, it is far better in the long run for the child to know that normal, healthy, sad adults cry too.

36 When children lose someone they love, life is no longer secure. The fact that parents can't prevent illness, accidents, and death all of the time is a realization the children must deal with. They must also accept the fact that they too will be parents someday and will not be able to protect their children from all harm.

37   Some children may suffer more from the loss of a sibling than from the loss of a parent because of the strong sibling bond from which a sibling draws so much of his or her own identity. A child may be much closer emotionally to a sibling than to parents if the parents work or travel a great deal. Also, a child may see their own death more clearly in the death of a sibling than in the death of a parent or other adult.

38   Children who lose a sibling may also lose their best friend, source of comparison and identity, protector, confidant, arguing partner, etc. This single loss may now become a multiple loss for the child. This is especially felt if the sibling loses a twin.

39 Fighting and squabbling among siblings seem to be almost needed, healthy forms of communication that children say they miss after the death of a sibling.

40 Sometimes it is not until after death that siblings will realize the depth of the bond they had with their dead brother or sister. Or, this may be a bond they did not realize even existed during the life of both. Or, they may regret that the bond was not stronger, and feel guilt or regret about that.

41 A death in a family will usually draw bereaved siblings closer together. If a parent, sibling, or other relative dies, the remaining siblings can relate to this as a similar loss that they are experiencing together, and they can draw support from each other.

42 When a child changes position in a family due to the death of a brother, sister or parent, this can cause even more stress and added problems. For example, going from the second oldest to the oldest can now place a new burden of responsibility on the child. In the case of a parent's death, an older child may have to take on added responsibilities. Becoming the only child because of a sibling loss is extremely hard also. There are no other siblings with whom to share one's grief.

43   Children may grieve severely over an infant's death . . . an infant they did not even know. They may have a harder time letting go of the *new baby* fantasy than a parent who has reality to deal with such as meals to cook and laundry to wash. Plus, their hopes and plans for the new brother or sister are now destroyed.

44   Children have a natural curiosity about siblings who died before they were born. Parents should not hesitate to share photos and memories with the child.

45 Surviving siblings may try to *become* their dead brother or sister to try to please their parents or to satisfy their own loss. They may begin to act and dress like the deceased, develop hobbies that the deceased had, wear their hair like the deceased, etc. To a certain extent, this can be normal grief behavior; but, if carried to extremes, it could be cause for alarm.

46 Chilren, oftentimes, when asked how many brothers or sisters they have, will not include the dead sibling to avoid embarrassing questions that may follow as a result. This is a normal response, and parents who have lost a child will often do the same thing when asked how many children they have.

47 Some children (usually teen-agers) have dreams or premonitions that something will happen to someone they love. This can be very frightening to them, and they may not say anything to anyone about it until after the death occurs. Then they may be consumed with guilt that they may have been able to prevent it had they said something.

48 Many children have dreams about their loved ones who have died. In their dreams they usually visit the dead person in heaven, or the dead person comes back to visit them. Pets that have died may also appear in these dreams. These dreams can be very comforting and re-assuring for children, and they should be encouraged to talk about them.

49   Children are not usually aware
that adults have many of the
same feelings that they do regarding grief . . . or that other
bereaved children share their
feelings. Grief has a way of
isolating young and old alike
into thinking they are the only
ones having these painful
feelings. Thus, there is a
tendency to try to endure
these feelings in silence.

50   Children need to know that
their feelings are normal grief
feelings, even though they may
not be normal under other circumstances. For instance, anger
at God or severe guilt is
normal. It is when these feelings persist for many months
that concern should be acted
upon.

51 Instead of grieving intensely for a year or so, children are more likely to grieve intermittently over many years. This is why so many adults think that children grieve very little, if at all.

52 In the frontier days, many children died because of disease, and it was not uncommon for children to be aware of and somewhat accepting of death. Then, our society went through several generations where childhood diseases were cured for the most part, and it was unthinkable, with modern medicine, for children to die. Now, we are back in an age when children are dying - the sad thing is that many of them are dying by their own hands because of drugs, gang wars and suicide.

53 Many bereaved children enter the world of drugs as a way to escape from having to deal with a significant loss. This loss could be the death of a loved one. On the other hand, it may not have anything to do with death – such as a divorce in the family, a loss of friendship, or a loss of self-esteem. You can't treat the drugs successfully without getting to the root of the problem, which is their reason for starting to use drugs to begin with.

54 Children grieve at their own pace just as they grow at their own pace. You cannot judge one child's recovery by the way other children have recovered under the same or similar circumstances.

55 Because society tends to rally around the adults when a family member dies, the children involved may consciously or unconsciously deny the validity of their own loss. They may see their own grief as not justifiable, and may not begin their own grief process for many years to come . . . or maybe never.

56 Unresolved grief can negatively influence bereaved children even into and throughout adult life, not only in their relation-ship with others, but in how they feel about themselves. Un-resolved anger and guilt can cause some individuals to feel they are bad people and thus unworthy of the love and re-spect of others. This can lead to poor self-esteem and low self-image.

57 Adults get a kick sometimes out of saying things in jest that make it sound like they want to get rid of their kids. This can be very hurtful and confusing if said to a bereaved child. . . be it their own child or one within earshot.

58 It is hard for bereaved siblings to hear other children say mean things about their own brothers and sisters such as, "I hate my brother!" or "My sister is a jerk."

59 Many bereaved children feel better if they can talk with another bereaved child. There is a sense of safety and security that this other person has been through the same or similar ex-perience and will understand. Children's self-help groups are flourishing throughout the coun-try, although at a slower pace than adult groups.

60 Children may ask a bereaved child questions that any adult would find abhorrent and shocking. For example, a question such as, "Are the worms crawling on your sister now?" may roll off a child's tongue with an innocence that is hard to believe. The child asking the question is not trying to be hateful or hurtful, but is simply exhibiting the inquisitive, uninhibited nature of a child.

61 When a child dies, other children must face the fact that even the young can die. This may be difficult for some children - especially teenagers - since they think they are, for the most part, invincible.

62 Because bad things happen to children when they are naughty, children may feel guilty because they equate the death or loss with being punished for something they did wrong. For example, a child may feel that their mother is divorcing their father because the child neglected to clean up his or her room when told to do so.

63 Sometimes children may use one word to describe a feeling when they really mean something else. For example, using the word *boring* to describe talking about a loss, when they really mean *painful* but don't want to admit it or can't admit it.

64 Children may have funny or scary feelings about the room or part of the house where the loved one died, and may not want to go near that part of the house. Respect their feelings and do not make them feel silly or dumb for feeling that way.

65 Like adults, bereaved children will also have times when they will rush into the deceased person's room or pick up the phone to call them - and then bingo - reality comes crashing in again. For a brief moment, it is as though the loved one were still alive.

66 It is possible that bereaved children had a less than loving relationship with the person who died, even though it may be someone as close as a parent, brother, or sister. In this case, their grief may truly be diminished, and they will recover from their grief quickly. Or maybe they are expected to mourn for a grandparent or other relative who they didn't know and really had no close feelings for. If it is no great loss to the child, then others should not try to make it be what it isn't.

67 Some children are angry at God and have a hard time working through this anger. Even a child who is raised in a religious family may question his or her religion and how it is going to help in this time of severe upheaval.

68 Because young children do not have the verbal skills to express their grief, other means of expression should be provided for them. Play-acting and drawing pictures are two excellent ways to accomplish this and should be done with the guidance of a parent or other adult. Sometimes a counsellor or therapist is recommended.

69 Bereaved children may wake up in the morning and for a brief moment forget that a death has occurred . . . then the loss will hit them like a ton of bricks and a great sadness will come over them. For this reason, bereaved children may have to go through an adjustment at the beginning of each new day and this may cause them to start off the day in a bad mood. Be understanding.

70 Some bereaved children may have make-believe conversations with the deceased. This is normal, and, again, is another way of feeling close to the loved one.

71 Bereaved children will despair, as do adults, at not being able to remember *exact* details about their loved one who died, such as the color of their eyes, the sound of their voice, the way they laughed. It is sad when these memories begin to fade, even if it is ever so slightly.

72 Like adults, children miss seeing what the future would have held for the loved one who died. They wonder such things as how tall they would have been, or if they would have been captain of the football team, or queen of the senior ball.

73 Sometimes bereaved children will become very hostile due to the frustration they have over the loss and not being able to change it. They may become anti-social and fight often with their friends. This will lead to more guilt, which leads to more anger and frustration, etc. Grief has a way of feeding on itself and perpetuating bad feelings.

74 Children may blame a parent, sibling, relative, doctor, etc., for their loved one's death. Affixing blame can be a normal stage in the grief process. After an extended period of time, it could be a serious problem and should be dealt with on a professional level whether the accusation is justified or not. Sometimes the accusation is true and it will be very hard for the child to learn to live with.

75 In some cases, the child is responsible for the death of his or her loved one and there is usually a large dose of "survivor's guilt" that follows. Survivor's guilt may also occur in the child even if the child was not responsible for the loved one's death. This is another situation where professional help is strongly suggested.

76 Children who are directly involved in the death of a loved one or who are at the scene of the death may have nightmares for many months thereafter. This is a situation where a professional counselor may be necessary to help them work through this.

77 A bereaved child may develop a fear of the dark that was not there before. Some of this fear may be due to nightmares, or the child may simply be very lonesome. If a child slept in the same room with a sibling who died, the dark room may have scary connotations. Because of all the horror movies and ghost tales to which children are subjected, it is no wonder some children experience these eerie feelings.

78 Some children withdraw and will not let themselves get close to others for fear of being hurt again. It is not uncommon for unresolved childhood grief to lead to self-destructive relationships as an adult.

79 Children have paradoxical feelings:
a. They like being hugged, but feel embarrassed when they are.
b. They are jealous of the child who died and went to heaven, but are afraid to die themselves.
c. They have more anger after a death, but are turned off by anger and violence in movies and television.

80 Sometimes children will have so much guilt and feel so bad about themselves and the loss that they will convince themselves the loved one died deliberately just to get away from them. A child needs reassurance that this is not true.

81 The way children relate cause and effect to events is not always rational or realistic. Thus, children may think they caused their loved one's death if they had a fight with them or wished them dead. They sometimes feel like they have an almost magical power to control what happens to others. Make sure a child knows that nothing he or she did caused the death. Do not assume children know this.

82 After a death, most children feel more vulnerable to something bad happening to them, their parents, or other loved ones. The "it can never happen to me" beliefs are shattered and replaced by feelings of "if it happened once, it can happen again."

83   Whenever possible, adults need to try to anticipate what guilt children might be feeling and assure them that they were not to blame. One thing is for sure about the grief process - there is always enough guilt to go around - and if a person doesn't have any, that person can always manufacture some, whether it is justified or not.

84   Some bereaved children actually feel like they look physically different . . . as if there is a big wart on the end of their nose. They may feel that everyone is staring at them when they walk into a classroom. This, in turn, will make them feel self-conscious and embarrassed.

85 Children may have to deal with incredibly hurtful and insensitive statements made to them regarding their loss. If a child tells another child that he had a brother or sister who died, he may easily be called a liar and ridiculed in front of his peers.

86 Most children say they feel guilty when they first start to laugh or have fun after the loss of someone they love. This is a normal reaction because there is a sense of guilt that you are abandoning the memory of the one who died. But laughing and having fun again are necessary parts of healing.

87 Some children want to be by themselves when they are sad. This "down time" is important and should be respected by adults and peers alike. Do not feel like you always have to be cheering them up and keeping them busy.

88 Often a later, less significant loss, such as the loss of a pet turtle, can open a floodgate of tears and grief. The bereaved child is really grieving over the loss of a significant *person* who died. Unconsciously, transfering this grief to a pet or inanimate object is far less threatening. This is as healthy a way as any for the child to get these painful feelings out.

89 To many, the strong feelings of grief in children are unbelievable and may thus be discounted. The term "the forgotten mourners" is often applied to grieving children because our society has been very slow to recognize that children do grieve, and with the same intensity as adults.

90 Bereaved children may get angry at the person who died for leaving them with so much pain and sorrow to have to live with. This is a very normal grief response for both children and adults, but it usually creates guilt for being angry at the person who died. Now, guilt is an added problem that has to be dealt with.

91 Cooperative and friendly children may become withdrawn and aggressive after a loss. These children may lash out at one of their peers or authority figure because they do not feel able to lash out at their parents for fear of causing them more pain if the parents are also grieving.

92 The ability of children to enter their own little fantasy world also allows them to resume play almost immediately or soon after a severe loss, much to adults' dismay. This is why you may see a child out riding a bicycle and playing with friends only hours after being told a loved one has died. This does not have anything to do with how much the child loved the deceased.

93 Even infants experience loss anxiety. If you don't believe this, just play "peek-a-boo" with a baby sometime. The infant usually starts to cry when you disappear and smile when you reappear.

94 Grief has a way of making one see things only in a negative light and remembering only the bad things that happened. If children are feeling guilty because they fought often with the deceased, it is important to get them to begin to focus on the good times they had with the deceased as well.

95 Children want their feelings to be acknowledged and understood . . . but not pitied. It embarrasses them if an adult makes a scene over their loss. A comforting hug or word is usually appreciated, although even this can be uncomfortable for some children.

96 Sudden deaths are usually harder for children to cope with because of feeling like they never really got to say goodbye.

97 Crying is therapeutic and a healthy way for bereaved children to show their grief. Crying should be encouraged. There is evidence to indicate that tears shed from sorrow are chemically different than other kinds of tears; they contain more toxic substances.

98 Children can sense that their friends feel uncomfortable when they begin to talk about their loved one who has died. Bereaved children usually will not force the conversation, with the end result being that they are often left with no one to share their painful feelings with.

99 Bereaved children who are denied the right to grieve the way they want to will sometimes compensate for this. For example, a young girl was refused permission to go to the grave site of her cousin, so she fashioned a grave in one corner of her room where she could place flowers whenever she liked.

100 Most bereaved children like to remember and talk about the deceased with friends and relatives. Unfortunately, there is a phenomenon called "the conspiracy of silence" that makes it difficult for others to talk about the dead person because they are afraid of hurting the bereaved person's feelings. The bereaved person, on the other hand, has hurt feelings when people won't talk about the deceased with them. It is a catch-22 situation.

101 Once children have experienced the death of someone close, they begin to question society's fascination with death and violence. Many bereaved children no longer enjoy scary stories and games. On the other hand, most children love being scared, and those who don't are made fun of by their peers. This can put bereaved children in an uncomfortable position at slumber parties, camp-outs, etc., if they are expected to take part in scary activities.

102 Children are greatly influenced by violence on TV and in the movies, even though they will deny that it affects them in a negative way. They truly may not realize that they are being adversely affected, because it is a subtle process that can occur over a long period of time. Also, peer pressure demands that a child act nonchalant – even flippant – regarding "media horror," lest they be teased or ridiculed by their friends.

By the time a child reaches the twelfth grade, he or she will have been exposed to more than 17,000 acts of violence through "entertainment mediums." This cannot help but lessen their sensitivity to the tragic reality of death, violence, and brutality.

103 It is not uncommon for some bereaved teenagers (or younger) to become suicidal, or at least become preoccupied with the possibility of suicide. In our present society, suicide has become a viable alternative to teenagers who cannot cope with the stress of losing a loved one, flunking math, or breaking up with a steady. Many have the sad notion that if they just *attempt* suicide and then are saved, they can get all of the sympathy and attention they want without actually having to die. This goes back to the unhealthy, distorted views we are giving our children about the tragedy of death.

104 Older bereaved children may immerse themselves in behavior that will prevent them from having to deal with the death, such as pouring themselves into their schoolwork or sports. Adults may do the same thing with their housework or office work. It creates a diversion and for short periods of time can be a positive behavior.

105 Older bereaved children may change some of their friends or even their whole circle of friends as a result of a loss. They will gravitate to those who give them comfort and understanding, and move away from those friends they no longer feel comfortable around. Often, this can be a very positive situation.

106 Some children may engage in potentially dangerous or fate-provoking behavior, either to punish themselves or to test their own mortality. For example, if someone they loved died in a car wreck, they may engage in reckless driving.

107 Some bereaved children will manipulate parents, teachers, etc., by faking the extent of their grief to get attention and sympathy. Extra doses of love and a few extra hugs usually cure these symptoms.

108 Reaching an age at which an older sibling died is frightening. It is a relief when bereaved children get through this age . . a psychological barrier has been broken. Some children will even go so far as to re-enact the way their older sibling died on that exact day and at the same time and place. For example, if an older sibling drowned in a pool, the younger sibling may deliberately swim in that same pool when he or she reaches that age, as a symbolic way of defying fate. In the case of suicide, there have even been documented cases where a younger sibling has committed suicide in the same manner when reaching the age of the older sibling who died, or on the anniversary date of the older sibling's death.

109   Some bereaved children perform "tie-breaking activities" as a way of working through their grief. Such things as putting some pictures away, dismantling the *shrine,* or replacing their dead brother's baseball glove in favor of a new one can be considered tie-breaking activities. These behaviors are normal and healthy.

110   Many bereaved children engage in behaviors which maintain a sense of continuity and safety. They are not as prone as adults to making drastic changes after a death, such as changing jobs or residences. Maybe this is because they are not as free as adults to make these types of major decisions.

111 Children may turn their dead sibling or parent into an idealized figure they feel they have to compete with or live up to. For example, a surviving sibling may feel that he or she now has to excel in sports or academics to be like the sibling who died. If a child feels that the pressure to compete is too great, that child may do just the opposite and become a school drop-out or choose some other form of deliberate failure.

112 It is not unusual for a child to take pleasure in wearing items of clothing or jewelry of the deceased. This is just a simple way of feeling close to the loved one who has died.

113   If the loved one died from an illness, any future illness can cause fear in children that they too will die from their illness. The illness the loved one died from should be explained to children as best they can understand, and reassurance given that not all illnesses cause death.

114   As much as possible, children should be included in the care and progress when a sick person close to them is terminally ill or about to die. This will allow them to get a head start on the grief process which is sure to follow.

115 Children have an intuitive sense regarding their own impending death. Research has proven that terminally ill children often know that they are going to die and when they are going to die long before they are told by their doctor or parents. It has even been proven that some children may have a feeling of an impending illness even before they are told they are sick. It is also a fact that they usually handle the news better than the parents do.

116 If parents have a terminally ill child, it is best for the parents to discuss the impending death with the child who is dying. These are very precious moments that need to be shared before it is too late.

117 Bereaved children may regress emotionally and developmentally by having tantrums, bedwetting, thumb sucking, clinging to parents, or wanting to be held constantly. Do not overreact. These are usually just temporary attempts to find comfort and safety.

118 A bereaved child is far more susceptible to physical ailments such as stomach aches, loss of appetite, lethargy, rashes, heightened allergic responses, colds, and even serious illnesses such as cancer. Because the immune system is weakened due to the stress caused by grief, it is very important to make sure that the bereaved child takes good physical care of himself or herself.

119 The knowledge and education of many pediatricians does not make their diagnoses foolproof. Many doctors still cannot spot a bereaved child processing his or her way through normal grief. Be careful of medications prescribed in place of love and understanding.

120 For many children, it is hard to go back to school after the loss of a loved one because of the unknown reactions they will get from classmates and teachers. They do not know if they will be swamped with sympathy or ignored altogether. It is important that "re-entering" is a positive experience for the the child, because a child's classmates may well be the closest social circle the child has.

121 Often the class is told not to talk about the death, so when the grieving child returns to the classroom and tries to pretend that nothing happened so they can fit in with the rest of the class - who are also pretending that nothing happened - the bereaved child is accused by his classmates of not caring about the person who died. When this misunderstanding occurs, it is often the school principal or a teacher who precipitates this painful situation, because they do not understand the needs of the grieving child or the needs of the classmates who may also be grieving. Death education in our schools would help to eliminate these types of problems for the faculty as well as the students.

122 Most children on going back to
school seem to feel better once
the class is told about the loss,
and acknowledgements are
made by both classmates and
teachers. Then the child does
not have to go through the
guessing games of "Do you
know?" or "Do they know I
know they know?" The opportunity is now open for the child
to talk with friends about the
loss and for the friends to express their sympathy and grief
as well.

123 After a death, children are expected to go back to school and maintain good grades. This is almost always impossible since their minds are preoccupied with the loss. Then, when the child sees grades slipping, this creates even more frustration and anxiety to add to the already difficult grief process.

124 Classes that require great concentration and detail such as math or chemistry may be the first ones to show a drop in grades for a bereaved child.

125 A parent should always inform the teacher if his or her child has suffered a recent significant loss; and this includes a divorce in the family. By the teacher being aware of this, potential problems can be avoided in the classroom. You are not protecting the child or doing the child a favor by keeping this information a secret.

126 Displaced grief can show up in totally unrelated behavior such as fighting with friends, disruptive behavior in the classroom, rebellion toward authority figures, learning disabilities, drugs, etc. Teachers should always be aware of students who have experienced an important loss.

127 An unintentional incident at school could trigger a landslide of grief that could result in the grieving child coming home very upset and agitated. It may have to do with a classroom assignment or an incident on the playground that caused some very painful feelings to surface regarding the deceased. Children should be encouraged to talk about the incident so they can, hopefully, understand it and feel better about it.

128 A child does not like to be singled out as an only child in the classroom or in front of their peers if the child became an only child by losing a brother or sister. All this does is emphasize the bereaved child's loss.

129 If a child has caused the death of a loved one, he or she is more than likely having to deal with being called awful names and being treated in a hateful manner by peers. Children can be very cruel and insensitive about things such as this. For example, the child who accidentally shoots his sister may be having to deal with his peers calling him a murderer or killer. Chances are the child may not tell anyone if this is happening, so parents and teachers should be on the look-out for this type of problem.

130 The number of children who are having to deal with the deaths of their peers is reaching alarming proportions, and many schools are not providing children with the coping skills to handle these serious losses. Children and faculty alike from first grade on would benefit greatly from organized, mandatory curriculum on death education.

131 Children are drawn together in situations of tragedy and will draw strength and support from each other. When a school-age child dies, the whole school should be allowed to grieve openly and together as a student body. Mourning *en masse* is as old as civilization itself, and has been practiced in even the lowest forms of civilization since the beginning of history.

132 Bereaved children who have worked through their grief are the best example for other children who are hurting and feeling hopeless. Many schools now have programs where children with successful grief coping skills can become peer counselors in helping positions. Many bereaved children grow up to be nurses, counselors, and others in care-giving fields as a result of their own personal grief experience.

133 If bereaved children indicate in any way that they *want* help or counseling, by all means, get it for them immediately. Most children are hesitant to openly request help that smacks of *formal counseling*. So, if this happens, consider it a blatant cry for help.

134 If professional counseling is needed for a bereaved child, be sure to take care in choosing the right counselor. Not all counselors have a healthy attitude about death or know how to counsel a grieving person. Some can even be harmful. Also, the counselor should be someone who the child feels comfortable with.

135 In the case where a child has died, studies show that the siblings whose parents belong to a grief-support group will fare better and go through their grief process more easily than those whose parents are not involved in a support group. This would probably be true in the case of any loss the family is suffering together. If the children see the parents getting help, then hopefully they will feel free to do the same.

136 Just because a child never talks about the dead person does not mean he or she is handling the death in a healthy way, or is over the grief process. In fact, it may mean just the opposite. The child should be encouraged to talk about the person who has died, but do not try to force a conversation because this almost never works.

137 Timing is of the essence in getting through to a bereaved child who needs help. You cannot make a bereaved child talk or be open to help if he or she doesn't want it; forcing the issue may cause a child to retreat even further.

138 Bereaved children look to adults as role models in learning how to cope with death in our society. Unfortunately, our society is one of the worst examples. Most adults are very uncomfortable with disease, illness, and death. We impart this uncomfortableness to our children - who will probably do the same with their children - unless the cycle of ignorance is broken.

139 Most bereaved children are not looking to adults to take away their grief as much as they are looking for validation of their grief and encouragement that they will get through it.

140 Some children are encouraged by well-meaning adults to be *extra good* when a loss has occurred in a family so as not to add to the burden of grief of the parents. The problem is that the children are probably grieving as severely in their own way and should not have to put their grief on the back burner while they help their parents.

141 Well-meaning friends and relatives may give a bereaved child advice about behavior that conflicts with the views or values of the child's parents. For example, the child may be encouraged by a relative to seek counseling, and the parents may be very opposed to professional help of any kind. This conflict can be very confusing and frustrating for the child.

142 Most taboos that children have about death are taught to them either intentionally or unintentionally by the adults around them. If children are taught at a very early age that death is a natural part of life, they will usually grow up with a healthy view of both life and death. Children who have a healthy view of death will value life as more precious, and the way they live their lives will reflect these values.

143 Children have a great deal of emotional strength that most adults do not give them credit for. Many children would fare far better than their adult counterparts were it not for the anxieties placed on them by the adults around them.

144 Bereaved children are usually more aware that life is precious and that the family is a gift to be cherished and not taken for granted.

145 Bereaved children usually mature faster than other children because they have faced grown-up issues early in life.

146 Bereaved children don't seem to fret as much over life's minor inconveniences as do other children. For the most part, they seem to have things more in perspective.

147 Bereaved children are generally more sensitive and compassionate than most children. They have experienced pain and suffering and are more aware of these feelings in others.

148 There is a strengthening effect on children who have experienced a serious loss and worked through it. They now have successful coping skills to get them through any future loss that might occur. We all experience loss of some type almost every day, and the coping skills that will get us through a death will also get us through the loss of a material item, a pet, or a job. The feelings of grief are the same with every loss. The intensity of the feelings is what is different.

149 Scott James Barrie gave himself a check mark every time he made his mother laugh and was proud when he could show the family physician five in one day. His mother was depressed over the death of his brother, David, age 14, the favorite son. Barrie later went on to write *Peter Pan.*

During his adolescence, Adolph Hitler regularly brooded at the window that overlooked his brother's grave.

Whether it sparks a turn to coping or psychopathology, sibling loss can leave an indelible mark on the developing child.

150 As they say in Alcoholics Anonymous, "A cucumber can become a pickle, but a pickle can never become a cucumber again." After a significant loss, every bereaved child is forever changed; forever different. In most cases, this is a positive change. They will never know the innocence that they knew before, but maybe this isn't all bad. Wiser for the experience, most bereaved children grow up to be wonderfully well-adjusted adults.

National Support Groups

American Council for Drug Education
6193 Executive Blvd.
Rockville, MD 20852

Bereaved Children's Group
8119 Holland Road
Alexandria, VA 22306

Brothers and Sisters Together
Miami Children's Hospital
6125 S.W. 31st Street
Miami, FL 33155

Center for Sibling Loss
Southern Human Services
1700 West Irving Park Road
Chicago, IL 60613

Children's Hospice International
501 Slaters Lane, Suite 207
Alexandria, VA 22314

Dougy Center
3909 SE 52nd
Portland, OR 97206

Fernside: A Center for Grieving Children
P.O. Box 8944
Cincinnati, OH 45208

Journey Program
> c/o Children's Hospital
> 4800 Sand Point Way
> Seattle, WA 98103

Kids Grieve Too
> c/o Hospice of the Red River Valley
> 1316 South 23rd Street
> Fargo, ND 58103

Missouri Baptist Hospital
> Department of Pastoral Care
> 3015 N. Ballas Road
> St. Louis, MO 63131

National Childhood Grief Institute
> 3300 Edinborough Way, Suite 512
> Minneapolis, MN 55435

National Committee on Youth Suicide Prevention
> 230 Park Ave., Suite 835
> New York, NY 10169

National Federation of Parents for Drug-free Youth
> 1820 Franwall Ave., Suite 16
> Silver Spring, MD 20902

National Sudden Infant Death Syndrome Foundation
> 2 Metro Plaza, Suite 205
> 8240 Professional Place
> Landover, MD 20785

Parents of Murdered Children
100 E. Eighth Street
Cincinnati, OH 45202

Pregnancy and Infant Loss Center
1415 E. Wayzata Boulevard #105
Wayzata, MN 55391

SHARE - St. John's Hospital
800 E. Carpenter St.
Springfield, IL 62769

Straight, Inc.
P.O. Box 21686
St. Petersburg, FL 33742

Survivors of Suicide, National Office
Suicide Prevention Center, Inc.
184 Salem Avenue
Dayton, OH 45406

The Compassionate Friends
P.O. Box 3696
Oak Brook, IL 60522-3696

The Good Grief Program
Judge Baker Guidance Center
295 Longwood Avenue
Boston, MA 02115

Other Books Published by:

**The Publishers Mark
P.O. Box 6300
Incline Village, NV 89450**

Linn, Erin. *Children Are Not Paper Dolls . . . a visit with bereaved siblings*; 1982

Linn, Erin. *I Know Just How You Feel . . . avoiding the cliches of grief*; 1986

Linn, Erin. *Dear Teacher*; 1988

Linn, Erin. *Premonitions, Visitations and Dreams . . . of the bereaved*; 1991